BIG ENGINEERING EXPERIMENTS

for little kids

A First Science Book for Ages 3 to 5

Dr. Jacie Maslyk

Illustrations by Tanya Emelyanova

**ROCKRIDGE
PRESS**

For my two little engineers, Caden and Tanner

Series Designer: Heather Krakora
Interior and Cover Designer: Regina Stadnik
Art Producer: Samantha Ulban
Editor: Barbara J. Isenberg
Production Editor: Mia Moran
Production Manager: Martin Worthington

Illustrations © 2021 Tanya Emelyanova
Author photo courtesy of Theresa Glenn Photography

ISBN: Print 978-1-64876-916-0
eBook 978-1-64876-917-7
R0

CONTENTS

FOR THE ADULT ENGINEERS

Thank you for introducing your child to the exciting world of engineering! Now more than ever, there is a need for creative thinkers and problem-solvers. It is important to teach young people how to communicate their unique thinking and collaborate with others to come up with solutions. Engineering provides a strong foundation for these skills—and it's fun!

The purpose of this book is to get young people excited about engineering. Hands-on discovery and play in early childhood are critical to the development of young learners. Not only can engineering build critical thinking and creativity skills, but it also helps develop fine and gross motor skills.

As your child's first teacher, you can support them as they engage in the excitement and inquiry connected to discovery learning. You can also foster learner development by allowing your child to engage in productive struggle. Try not to quickly interject with solutions when your child is having difficulty, but allow your child to fail and try again. That is the engineering design process in action.

While your child will need your support at times (we will include a CAUTION symbol when your assistance is needed ⚠️), we encourage you to let your child take the lead on everything from setup to cleanup. Each activity has a material list that features everyday items your child should be able to gather on their own.

Each activity wraps up with a brief explanation of "How It Works" and includes BIG vocabulary words for our smallest engineers. Questions and prompts about what your child has observed will help encourage them to explore further. There is a little engineer in every young child. This book will help it come out!

KID ENGINEER!

Are you ready to have some fun? In this book, you are going to become an engineer. Engineers are people who design things. They help figure out the best way to build skyscrapers, bridges, computers, and rockets. Some engineers even invent things! When they work, they follow something called the engineering design process. This means they go through these 5 steps to complete a project:

1. **ASK:** Engineers ask lots of questions. How does that work? Can I make it work better?

2. **IMAGINE:** The engineers think about possible answers to the questions.

3. **PLAN:** Then engineers make a plan by writing down or drawing their ideas.

4. **CREATE:** Once they have a plan, engineers begin to build. They try different materials and test different designs.

5. **IMPROVE:** Sometimes the plan doesn't work. The engineers try again to make their design better.

If you like to have fun with different materials, learn how things work, and build things, then you are ready to try some engineering. Ready, set, go!

Make It Move

Experiment time: 10 minutes

How can you make an empty can move without touching it?

Empty soda can   Balloon

Place an empty soda can on a hard, flat surface, like your kitchen floor.

Blow up the balloon. Ask an adult engineer to tie the balloon.

Rub the balloon on your hair for 15 seconds.

4

Place the balloon close to the can, but don't touch it.

BE CURIOUS

What happened when the balloon got close to the can? Can the balloon move other items? Try the experiment with a full soda can, an empty plastic water bottle, and other objects from around the house. Which items could the balloon move? What is the same about all those items?

HOW IT WORKS

Rubbing the balloon on your hair creates static electricity. This is a type of electric charge that is caused by friction (when something moves against something else). Static electricity can pull something toward an object or push it away. Computer engineers need to be aware of static electricity. It can damage or break computer parts.

MESSY METER

Build a Chair

WHAT YOU NEED

2 pipe cleaners   Small toy that can sit

Bend a pipe cleaner into a rectangle shape and twist the ends together.

Bend the rectangle into an L shape as shown.

Bend the tall side down. This is your chair's seat.

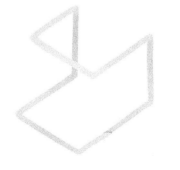

4

4

Make a rectangle with the second pipe cleaner, just like you did in step 1.

5

Slide the new rectangle between the "arms" of the bent pipe cleaner as shown. This is the back of the chair.

6

Place your toy in its new chair!

BE CURIOUS

Does the chair hold your toy? Why or why not? How could you design a bigger chair? What shapes or materials would you use? Try using more pipe cleaners to make a new, stronger chair design. What pieces can you change to make the chair stronger?

HOW IT WORKS

Civil engineers build things like roads, bridges, and buildings. They use geometry (the study of shapes) to solve problems. These engineers try different shapes to find out which shape works best for a project. The base of your chair is a rectangle. The rectangle shape works in this case because the design uses force (the push or pull on an object) to keep your toy in the chair.

MESSY METER

Make It Melt

· WHAT YOU NEED ·

Ice cube

Bowl or dish

Salt shaker filled with
table salt

Timer

1

Place the ice cube in a bowl or dish.

2

Shake the salt shaker 10 times over the ice cube.

3

Set the timer for 2 minutes.

4

4

After 2 minutes, notice what happened to the ice cube. How does it look different?

5

Then add 10 more shakes of salt to the ice cube.

BE CURIOUS

How did the salt change the ice cube? What else can you put on the ice cube? Ask an adult engineer if you can use rubbing alcohol, sugar, or baking soda ⚠. Which melted the ice fastest? Which melted the ice slowest?

HOW IT WORKS

Salt lowers the freezing point of water. This is the temperature water needs to turn into ice (32 degrees Fahrenheit). When ice reaches a temperature higher than the freezing point, it starts to melt. Since salty ice needs to be much colder to stay frozen, it melts at 32 degrees Fahrenheit. Adding more salt makes the ice melt faster.

MESSY METER

Penny Boats

Experiment time: 20 minutes

How can you turn a sheet of aluminum foil into a boat that keeps pennies afloat?

WHAT YOU NEED

12-inch ruler

Aluminum foil

Large bowl of water

50 pennies

Use your ruler to measure about 12 inches of aluminum foil. Then ask an adult engineer to cut it from the roll.

Place the piece of foil on a hard, flat surface and fold the sheet in half by matching the edges together.

Smooth out the foil. Then fold it in half again to make a square.

4

Carefully fold up all the edges of the foil to make the sides of your boat.

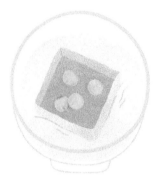

Put your boat into the bowl of water (or a sink or bathtub) and add a few pennies to the boat. Does your boat keep floating?

BE CURIOUS

How many pennies do you think you can add before your boat will sink? One by one, count the pennies as you put them in your boat. Can your boat hold all 50 pennies without sinking? Design a smaller boat. How many pennies can it hold?

HOW IT WORKS

The foil boat has less density than the water. Density tells us how much "stuff" is packed into an object. If you had a hollow rubber ball and a rock that were the same size, the rock would be heavier because it is more dense. Things float when they have less density than water, and sink when they have more.

MESSY METER

Playdough Pyramid

Experiment time: 20 minutes

How can you build a pyramid using 8 toothpicks?

············· **WHAT YOU NEED** ·············

Playdough

8 toothpicks

Make 5 small balls with the playdough. Each should be about the size of the tip of your thumb.

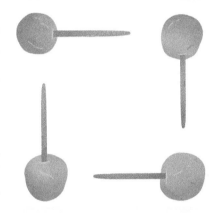

Make a square using 4 toothpicks and 4 balls of playdough as shown.

Keep the square flat on the table. Add 1 toothpick pointing upward from each corner of the square.

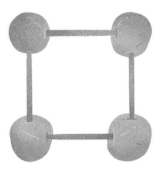

4

4

Push all 4 toothpicks so they meet in the center.

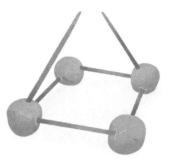

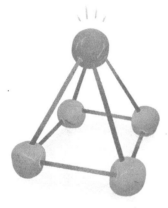

5

Use your last ball of play-dough to hold them together to make the top point of the pyramid.

BE CURIOUS

What shape did you create? What shapes is it made of? Can you make other shapes? Try one with 5 sides or 6 sides. How could you build a taller or longer shape using more toothpicks and playdough?

HOW IT WORKS

When you made the square, it was two-dimensional (2D). This means it was flat on the table. When you built upward, you made a three-dimensional (3D) pyramid shape. Engineers take 2D plans and turn them into 3D objects.

MESSY METER

Blow It Up!

Experiment time: 15 minutes

How can you fill a balloon with air without blowing into it?

········ WHAT YOU NEED ········

Funnel

Baking soda

Teaspoon-size
measuring spoon

Empty plastic water
bottle, 16 to 20 ounces

White vinegar

Balloon

Using the funnel, ask your adult engineer to measure 5 teaspoons of baking soda and carefully put it into the bottle.

Using the funnel again, ask your adult engineer to pour about ½ cup of the white vinegar into the bottle.

Quickly cover the top of the bottle with the open end of the balloon.

Carefully swirl the liquid in the bottle.

Watch the balloon expand!

BE CURIOUS

What happened to the balloon? What happened to the baking soda and vinegar? Why should an engineer know what happens when 2 materials are mixed together? Try the same experiment with a 2-liter bottle. Use 2 cups of vinegar and 10 teaspoons of baking soda. Do you think anything will be different?

HOW IT WORKS

When the baking soda and vinegar mixed together, there was a chemical reaction. The reaction made something new—a gas! The gas filled the bottle and had nowhere to go, so it blew up the balloon!

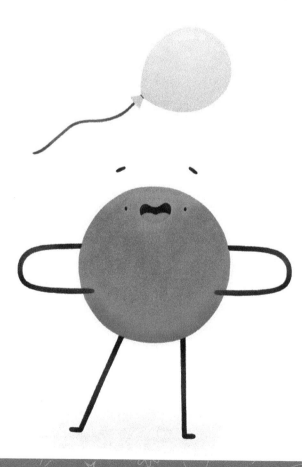

MESSY METER

Build a Bridge

Experiment time: 20 minutes

How can you build a spaghetti bridge to connect 2 chairs?

About
20 spaghetti noodles

About 20 mini
marshmallows

2 chairs (about
18 to 20 inches apart)

Ask an adult engineer to help you cut or break 13 pieces of spaghetti in half to make 26 smaller pieces.

Use a marshmallow to connect 1 long piece of spaghetti and 1 short piece. The pieces should form an L shape.

Use 2 marshmallows to add a short piece of spaghetti to form a triangle in the corner. Then connect another long piece of spaghetti.

4

Make an X by using another short piece of spaghetti and a marshmallow. Then use a short piece of spaghetti to connect the 2 long pieces.

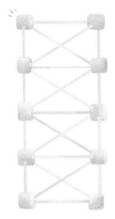

5

Repeat steps 2 and 3 until you get to the end of the long pieces of spaghetti. You should be able to make 4 Xs. This is half of your bridge.

6

Repeat steps 2 through 4 to make the other half of your bridge. Connect the 2 bridge halves with marshmallows. Now put your bridge between the 2 chairs!

BE CURIOUS

What did you notice when you placed your bridge between the chairs? Try using more X shapes to make your bridge stronger. Where should you attach them? In the middle? On the ends? Can you design and build a bridge strong enough to hold a small stuffed animal?

HOW IT WORKS

Using X shapes in the bridge design helped make the bridge more stable. Something that is stable is harder to break or bend. The X shapes formed a bunch of triangles in your bridge. Triangles work together to create a stronger bridge.

Steady Stacking

Experiment time: 15 minutes

How can you stack 15 cups to form a tower?

WHAT YOU NEED

15 plastic cups

Place 5 plastic cups face-down on the floor in a line.

Carefully balance 4 cups on top of the first cups to make a second level.

Use 3 cups to add another level.

4

Add 2 cups to form the next level of your tower.

5

Carefully add the last cup to the very top of your tower.

BE CURIOUS

What did you notice as you were building? How many cups would you need to build your tower if you started with 7 cups on the first level? Can you build a cup tower that is as tall as you? How many cups should you start with? How many will you need in all?

HOW IT WORKS

The cups will only stack if you carefully balance them between the 2 cups below. Balance means that the weight of the cups is shared evenly, so that the tower can stand tall and steady. This is an important thing for engineers to remember when they are designing a building.

MESSY METER

Up in the Air

Experiment time: 20 minutes

How can you make a parachute that works for one of your toys?

.... **WHAT YOU NEED** ....

Tissue paper

Ruler

Scissors

Hole punch

Lightweight string

Small toy or action figure

Ask an adult engineer to measure and cut a piece of tissue paper into a 12-inch square.

Use the hole punch to make 1 hole in each corner of your tissue paper.

Ask an adult engineer to cut 4 (12-inch) pieces of string.

4

Tie 1 piece of string through each hole. Ask an adult engineer if you need help.

Take 2 loose strings from one side of the paper and tie the bottoms together. Do the same with the other 2 strings.

Place the 2 large loops that you made under the arms of your action figure. Toss your toy into the air and watch what happens!

BE CURIOUS

What happened to your toy after you tossed it into the air? What might happen if you put a hole in the center of your parachute? How well would the parachute work if it was bigger or smaller? Try using a plastic grocery bag or a paper towel to make a parachute ⚠. Which material worked the best? Why?

HOW IT WORKS

The parachute creates something called air resistance when the toy is falling. The air pushes against the parachute and slows the toy from falling. The bigger the parachute, the more air resistance it will create, and the slower the toy will fall.

MESSY METER

Racing Ramps

Experiment time: 10 minutes

How can you make a toy car move faster down a ramp?

········· **WHAT YOU NEED** ·········

Long piece of cardboard   5 thick books   Toy car

Place one end of the card-board on a book. Let the car roll down the ramp. Don't push it.

Add a second book, then put the cardboard on top. Try rolling the car again.

Add a third book to the stack and send the car down the ramp.

4

4

Now place a fourth book on the pile and let the car speed down the ramp.

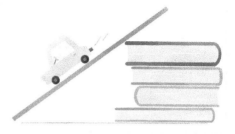

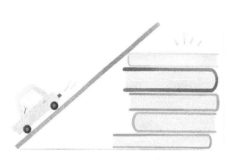

5

Place the fifth book onto the pile. *Vrooom* goes your car!

BE CURIOUS

What did you notice as you added each book to the stack? Did the car move faster or slower? Why? What would happen if you added even more books? Make 2 ramps using books and cardboard and race 2 cars down the ramps. Which car won the race? Why?

HOW IT WORKS

The higher you make the stack of books, the steeper the ramp gets. The steeper the ramp, the faster the car will go. You might notice this if you are on a bike or scooter. It is much easier to move faster going downhill.

MESSY METER

Jumping Pepper

Experiment time: 10 minutes

How can you use a comb to grab pepper out of a salt and pepper mixture?

. . . . **WHAT YOU NEED** . . . .

Salt

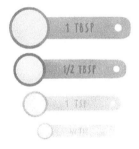

Measuring spoons

Bowl

Black pepper

Plastic comb

Measure and put
2 tablespoons of salt into
the bowl.

Add ½ teaspoon of pepper
to the bowl.

Gently shake the bowl to mix
the salt and pepper together.

4

Run the plastic comb through your hair at least 5 times.

5

Hold the comb very close to the salt and pepper. Watch what happens!

BE CURIOUS

What happened when you put the comb near the salt and pepper? What might happen if you added more pepper? Would it still jump to the comb? Set up another experiment to see if the comb can move a tissue, plastic grocery bag, rubber ball, or string ⚠.

HOW IT WORKS

When you run the comb through your hair, it creates a static charge. You used this same charge to move the empty soda can earlier in this book (see Make It Move on page 1). The pepper reacts more to the charge than the salt, so it jumps to the comb. Energy can be created and used in engineering. Engineers need to know how to use energy to power things like machines, vehicles, and even towns.

MESSY METER

Ready for Takeoff!

Experiment time: 10 minutes

How can you make a paper airplane that flies?

Piece of 8½-x-11-inch paper

1

Fold the paper in half so both long edges touch.

2

Fold down one corner to make a triangle as shown. Flip over the paper and do the same thing. This will be the nose of your plane.

3

Carefully fold down one wing by lining it up with the bottom of the paper as you see here.

4

Flip over the paper and make the same fold on the other side.

5

Unfold the wings a little so they stick out. Hold the nose of your plane and gently toss the plane forward.

BE CURIOUS

How long did your plane fly before it crashed? Put a paper clip on the nose of your plane. Does this change anything? Try using tape to hold the folds in place and add tape to the point of the nose. Do these changes help your plane fly farther?

HOW IT WORKS

Paper airplanes use forces called lift and thrust to fly. Lift is what keeps the plane off the ground. Thrust is what moves it forward. When these forces are balanced, a paper airplane will fly longer. Your hand gives the plane thrust, and the wings give it lift.

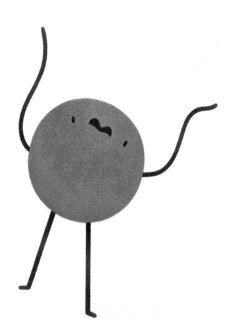

MESSY METER

Up and Down

Experiment time: 15 minutes

You are an engineer working on a tall building. How will you get the supplies you need to the top of the building?

WHAT YOU NEED

String or yarn

Scissors

Ruler

Small paper cup

Cellophane tape

Ask an adult engineer to cut a long piece of string (about 36 inches).

Tie the ends of the string together. You can ask an adult engineer to help.

Attach the string to the inside of the paper cup with tape as shown.

4

Place the string (and attached cup) around a doorknob.

5

Pull down on the side of the string without the cup. You are seeing a pulley in action!

BE CURIOUS

What happened when you pulled the string? What happens when you pull the other side? Put different things in the cup and lift them with your pulley. Can your pulley move some paper clips? Pennies? How about a heavy rock?

HOW IT WORKS

When you pull down on one side of a pulley, the other side goes up. Pulleys make it much easier to lift heavy objects. The object the pulley is lifting is called the load. Engineers designed elevators, cranes, and garage doors using pulleys!

Making Music

Experiment time: 5 minutes

How can you make a drinking straw into a musical instrument?

WHAT YOU NEED

Plastic drinking straw

Scissors

Ask an adult engineer to carefully snip off a small piece of one end of the straw at an angle as shown.

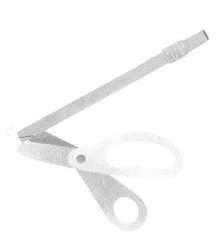

Make the same cut on the other side so the end of the straw comes to a point as you see here.

Flatten the opening of the other end of the straw with your thumb and finger.

4

4

Blow through the flattened end of the straw.

BE CURIOUS

What did you hear when you blew through the straw? Is there a different sound if you blow softly or more forcefully? What other types of noises can you create with things around the house? Can you find something to use as a drum or a shaker?

HOW IT WORKS

When you blew through the straw, the air caused the cut end of the straw to move. These movements are called vibrations. When things vibrate, they can create sounds. Vibrations are all around us. Engineers who build buildings need to understand how vibrations can impact their designs. They must create strong structures that can withstand vibrations from severe weather, like tornadoes and earthquakes.

MESSY METER

Rocket Balloon

Experiment time: 20 minutes

How can you make a balloon travel on its own across a string?

.... **WHAT YOU NEED** ....

String

Scissors

Ruler

Cellophane tape

Drinking straw

Balloon

Ask an adult engineer to cut a piece of string that is about 4 feet long (taller than you!).

Tape the straw to the balloon so that the open end of the balloon is facing the same way as one end of the straw.

Thread the string through the straw.

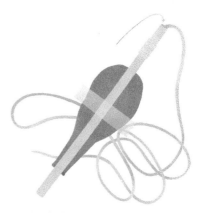

Tie one end of the string to the back of a chair.

Blow up the balloon and keep the end pinched closed. Move the balloon to the end of the string. Let go of the balloon!

BE CURIOUS

What happened when you let go of the balloon? Try lowering the end of the string before letting the balloon go. What happens? Blow up the balloon even bigger. Did it act the same on the string?

HOW IT WORKS

When you blow up the balloon, the air creates pressure inside the balloon. This means that the air is trapped and wants to get out. When you let the air out of the balloon, the air rushes out quickly. The force of the moving air pushes the balloon and straw forward—across the string. This is the same way a rocket works!

MESSY METER

Sink or Float?

Experiment time: 5 minutes

Will a ketchup packet sink or float?

Ketchup packet
(mayonnaise, mustard,
or any condiment
packet will work)

Empty clear water
bottle with cap
(16 to 20 ounces)

Water

Place the ketchup packet
inside the empty water bottle.

Slowly pour the water into
the empty bottle until it is full.

Twist the cap onto the filled
bottle. An adult engineer
can help.

Slowly turn the water bottle upside down. Watch what happens to the packet.

BE CURIOUS

What happened to the packet when you filled the bottle with water? What happened when you turned the bottle upside down? Hold the middle of the bottle, squeeze, then let it go. What happens when you squeeze? What happens when you let go?

HOW IT WORKS

There is a little bit of air inside the ketchup packet. This makes it float. This means the packet is buoyant. Buoyancy is the force that makes things of all sizes float. Balls, boats, and even you can float because of buoyancy. Engineers who design submarines need to figure out how to use buoyancy to create a boat that can sink or float.

MESSY METER

Paper Pillars

Experiment time: 15 minutes

How can you hold a book off the ground using just 4 pieces of paper?

······· **WHAT YOU NEED** ···········

4 sheets of paper

Cellophane tape

Book

Roll 1 sheet of paper the long way into a tube shape (about as thick as 2 of your fingers).

Place a piece of tape in the middle of the tube so it stays rolled up.

Stand up the tube on a hard, flat surface. Now it is a pillar!

4

Repeat steps 1 through 3 to make 3 more tubes. Stand them up so they make a square shape about the size of your book.

Carefully place the book on top of the pillars.

BE CURIOUS

Did the paper pillars hold up the book? Try adding more books on top. How many books did your pillars hold before breaking? Try rolling your paper tubes tighter or looser. Does this change how many books they can hold? What if you place the pillars closer together or farther apart?

HOW IT WORKS

The 4 paper pillars work together to share the load. The load is the weight that is being supported by the paper pillars. The stronger the pillars, the more of a load they can hold.

MESSY METER

Ding-Dong

Experiment time: 15 minutes

Can sound move through your body?

········· **WHAT YOU NEED** ·················

String

Scissors

Ruler

Metal clothes hanger

Ask an adult engineer to cut 2 (20-inch) pieces of string.

Tie 1 piece of string to one corner of the metal hanger. Ask an adult engineer for help if you need it.

Tie the other piece of string to the other corner of the hanger.

4

4

Wrap 1 loose end of string around each of your pointer fingers.

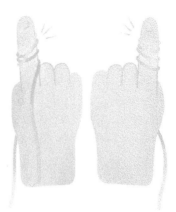

5

Put 1 pointer finger in each of your ears. The hanger should be hanging in front of you. Let the hanger gently bump into things around you (a table, a bookcase, a couch).

BE CURIOUS

What happens when the hanger bumps into hard things? Is it different than when it bumps into soft things? Are the sounds loud, soft, long, or short? What happens when someone taps the hanger with a spoon, a pencil, or a plastic straw?

HOW IT WORKS

When the hanger hits a hard object, it makes the metal vibrate. This makes sound waves. The sound waves move through the string, to your fingers, and into your ear. Then you hear the sound! Sound waves move through different objects. Engineers who work on airplanes, bridges, or boats will need to understand how sound travels. For example, airplane engineers need to design mechanical systems that are quiet for people traveling in the air.

MESSY METER

All Fall Down

Experiment time: 15 minutes

How can you knock over 5 books by only touching 1?

· · · · · · · · · · · · **WHAT YOU NEED** · · · · · · · · · ·

5 hardcover books
(or wooden blocks,
dominoes, or
shoeboxes)

Stand up 1 book on a hard, flat surface (like the floor).

Place a second book about 3 inches away from the first book. You are going to make a straight line of books.

Place the third book the same distance from the last book.

4

4

Put the fourth book in line with the others.

5

Once you put the fifth book in the line, gently push over the first book so it hits the book next to it.

BE CURIOUS

What happened to the books when you pushed the first book? What happens if you line up 10 books? Try placing a plastic cup at the end of your line of books. Put a small ball inside the cup. Can your reaction knock down the cup so the ball rolls out?

HOW IT WORKS

You just made a chain reaction happen! A chain reaction is when one thing makes something happen and then that thing makes something else happen. When you tapped the first book, it caused all the other books to fall down.

MESSY METER

Magnet Magic

Experiment time: 35 minutes (includes glue-drying time)

How do metal things act around a magnet?

· · · · · · · · · · · · · · **WHAT YOU NEED** · · · · · · · · · · · · · ·

Ruler (or a wooden paint stirrer)

Magnet

Cellophane tape

Feather

Glue

Small paper clip

Put the magnet on the end of the ruler.

Tape the magnet to the ruler. This will be your magic wand.

Put 1 drop of glue on the feather.

Place the paper clip onto the glue dot. Add another drop on top of the paper clip.

Let the glue dry. Be patient. This may take up to 30 minutes.

Take your magic wand, say some magic words, and wave the wand near the feather.

BE CURIOUS

What happened when you waved the wand over the feather? Does your wand stick to the refrigerator? How about to a fork? Will your wand lift a coin? A safety pin? A piece of paper? What things won't the wand stick to?

HOW IT WORKS

The magnet on the ruler attracts other things that are made of metal. This means the magnet pulls objects to it. The metal of the paper clip is pulled by the magnet. This lets you lift the feather. Engineers use magnets to solve problems in construction, since magnets are a part of cranes and conveyor belts. Engineers also use magnets in outer space when they work with satellites and spacecrafts.

ABOUT THE AUTHOR

An educator for the last 23 years, **Dr. Jacie Maslyk** has served as a classroom teacher, reading specialist, elementary principal, and assistant superintendent. She is passionate about STEAM education and the power of hands-on learning. She is the author of *STEAM Makers: Fostering Creativity and Innovation in the Elementary Classroom*, *Remake Literacy: Innovative Instructional Strategies for Maker Learning*, and *Unlock Creativity: Opening a World of Imagination with Your Students*. You can contact Jacie at jaciemaslyk@gmail.com or through her website STEAM-Makers.com.

ABOUT THE ILLUSTRATOR

Tanya Emelyanova was born in Siberia, where she studied advertising and mass communication. But since drawing has always been her true passion, she embarked on an illustration and pattern design career. Now she is working from her home studio in St. Petersburg, Russia. Tanya loves to create cute and funny characters and illustrations for children's books and magazines, printed art, and more, combining both digital and analog material.

CPSIA information can be obtained
at www.ICGtesting.com
Printed in the USA
JSHW061626070323
38553JS00002B/4